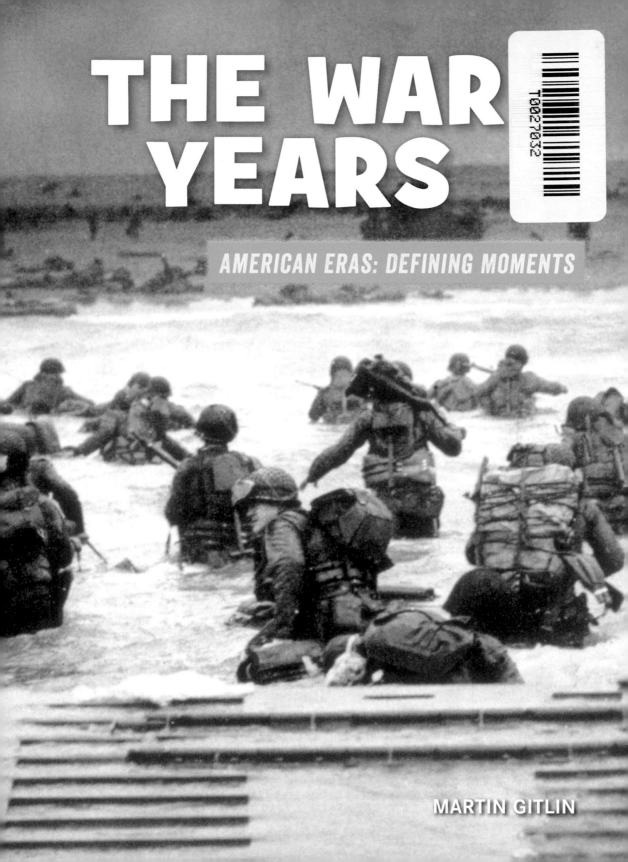

THE WAR YEARS

AMERICAN ERAS: DEFINING MOMENTS

MARTIN GITLIN

CHERRY LAKE PRESS

Published in the United States of America by Cherry Lake Publishing Group
Ann Arbor, Michigan
www.cherrylakepublishing.com

Content Adviser: Kevin Whinnery, MA, History
Reading Adviser: Beth Walker Gambro, MS, Ed., Reading Consultant, Yorkville, IL
Photo Credits: © Everett Collection/Shutterstock, cover, 1; © Library of Congress/LOC Control NO.
    2003652906, 5; © Everett Collection/Shutterstock, 7; © Photo by Clem Albers/Library of Congress/
    LOC Control No. 2001697374, 8; © Uploaded by Roke/Wikimedia, 11; © Keith Tarrier/Shutterstock, 12;
    © Photo by U.S. Maritime Commission/Library of Congress/LOC Control No. 94505434, 13;
    © Everett Collection/Shutterstock, 14; © Everett Collection/Shutterstock, 17; © Photo by Howard R.
    Hollem/Library of Congress/LOC Control No. 2017694372, 18; © Photo by Howard R. Hollem/Library
    of Congress/LOC Control No. 2017694377, 19; © Photo by Joseph A. Horne/Library of Congress/
    LOC Control No. 2017854777, 20; © Official U.S. Navy photo/Library of Congress/LOC Control No.
    92500933, 23; © Photo by U.S. Marine Corps/Wikimedia, 24; © Everett Collection/Shutterstock, 26;
    © Everett Collection/Shutterstock, 28

Library of Congress Cataloging-in-Publication Data
Names: Gitlin, Marty, author.
Title: The war years / by Martin Gitlin.
Description: Ann Arbor, Michigan : Cherry Lake Publishing Group, [2022] | Series: American eras:
    defining moments | Includes bibliographical and references index.
Identifiers: LCCN 2021007872 (print) | LCCN 2021007873 (ebook) | ISBN 9781534187382 (hardcover) |
    ISBN 9781534188785 (paperback) | ISBN 9781534190184 (pdf) | ISBN 9781534191587 (ebook)
Subjects: LCSH: World War, 1939-1945—United States—Juvenile literature. | United States—History—
    1933-1945—Juvenile literature.
Classification: LCC D769.1 .G568 2022 (print) | LCC D769.1 (ebook) | DDC 940.53/73—dc23
LC record available at https://lccn.loc.gov/2021007872
LC ebook record available at https://lccn.loc.gov/2021007873

Cherry Lake Publishing Group would like to acknowledge the work of the Partnership for 21st Century
Learning, a Network of Battelle for Kids. Please visit http://www.battelleforkids.org/networks/p21
for more information.

Printed in the United States of America
Corporate Graphics

ABOUT THE AUTHOR

Martin Gitlin has written more than 150 educational books. He also won more than 45 awards
during his 11-year career as a newspaper journalist. Gitlin lives in Cleveland, Ohio.

TABLE OF CONTENTS

INTRODUCTION

One crisis followed another in the late 1930s. The United States finally overcame the Great Depression in 1939. But the events in Europe and Asia were threatening to drag the nation into war.

A brutal form of government called **fascism** in Germany and Italy put the world in danger. German **dictator** Adolf Hitler proved the most dangerous. The **Nazi** leader used extreme violence to wipe out all opposition. He built a large political following by using the media to influence and prey on people's thoughts and feelings. Many people believed in his extreme message of **racism** and **anti-Semitism**. Germany launched an attack on Poland on September 1, 1939. It destroyed that country in a matter of weeks with fast-moving tanks and constant bombing from the skies, a furious type of warfare they called "lightning war," or *blitzkrieg*.

Hitler's armies had rolled over France and moved deep into Russia by the summer of 1941. Meanwhile, Great Britain was being pounded by German bombs.

Great Britain and France responded to the attack on Poland by declaring war on Germany on September 3, 1939.

Many Americans felt their country couldn't sit by and allow Germany to control Europe. Others wanted the United States to remain out of Europe and felt that it would be foolish to join another foreign war. They were known as **isolationists**.

But Germany wasn't the only danger. Japan was looking to expand its empire. The country had attacked China in 1937. Some believed that Japan also wanted war against the United States. Their worries proved correct. The United States was about to be dragged into World War II.

CHAPTER 1

A Horrible Sunday Surprise

The United States had remained out of World War II heading into December 1941. The country provided Britain with war supplies. But that was the extent of the United States' help. At the time, U.S. soldiers weren't being sent into battle.

That ended early on a Sunday morning. The date was December 7, 1941. The site was the Pearl Harbor naval base in Hawaii. Sailors woke up to the sound of Japanese planes. The Japanese were attacking Pearl Harbor. They wanted to destroy the United States' Pacific fleet before it could be used against them.

U.S. seamen scrambled to the decks to fight back. They shot at Japanese planes. But it was too late. The damage was done.

The Pearl Harbor attack lasted about 1 hour and 15 minutes.

Nearly 3,600 Americans were killed or wounded. Six ships and 169 planes were completely destroyed.

The surprise attack angered Americans. But it unified them in **patriotic** pride. They were pushed to action. Leading the charge was President Franklin D. Roosevelt. He made a speech to the U.S. Congress the very next day. Roosevelt referred to December 7 as "a date that will live in infamy." That afternoon on December 8, 1941, Congress declared war on Japan.

Over 120,000 Japanese Americans were placed in internment camps.

But it wasn't only Japan with whom the American people were at war. Soon, Germany declared war on the United States as well. The United States was officially at war in both Europe and Asia. The American people officially entered World War II. From soldiers overseas and Americans at home, great **sacrifice** would be required to help save the world.

A Shameful Chapter

Executive Order 9066 was signed on February 19, 1942. And it was made out of fear 2 months after the Japanese bombing of Pearl Harbor. The order sent Japanese Americans living anywhere near the West Coast to **internment** camps for the duration of World War II. The people it targeted lost their homes and businesses. But they had been as patriotic and loyal as any other Americans. Learn more about the internment of Japanese Americans during the war. Research actions Americans could have taken to reverse this decision. What would you have done?

CHAPTER 2

The War in Europe

The U.S. military faced an enormous challenge in Western Europe. Nazi Germany had **conquered** France. Russia, then part of the **Soviet Union**, was busy defending its own country. Italy, however, was fighting alongside the Nazis. Only Great Britain remained free among European forces.

About 150,000 American troops arrived in Europe from January to March 1942. More poured in during the next 3 years. In 1944, about 250,000 U.S. soldiers were sent to the European front each month.

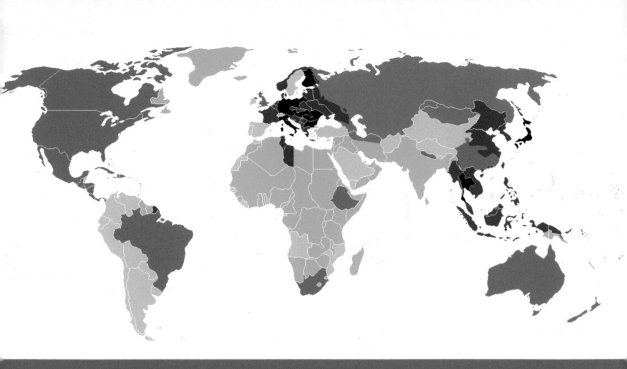

All but 16 countries took a side in the war.

The first task was defeating Nazi forces in North Africa. Only then could the Allied forces led by the United States and Britain free Europe.

Bloody battles were waged in North Africa. U.S. Army General Dwight Eisenhower and General George Patton joined British troops to subdue the Nazi Germans. That led to an invasion of key spots in southern Italy. That country was defeated on June 4, 1944.

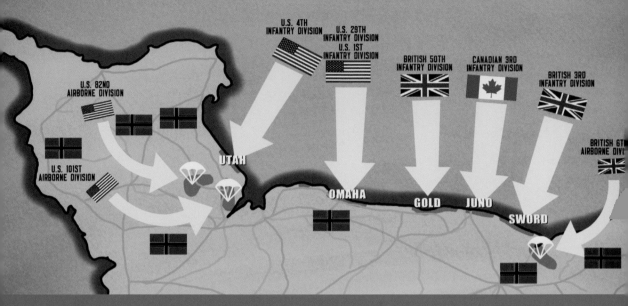

D-DAY INVASION MAP
JUNE 6TH 1944

Scale
10km

U.S. 4TH INFANTRY DIVISION
U.S. 29TH INFANTRY DIVISION
U.S. 1ST INFANTRY DIVISION
BRITISH 50TH INFANTRY DIVISION
CANADIAN 3RD INFANTRY DIVISION
BRITISH 3RD INFANTRY DIVISION
U.S. 82ND AIRBORNE DIVISION
BRITISH 6TH AIRBORNE DIVI
U.S. 101ST AIRBORNE DIVISION
UTAH
OMAHA
GOLD
JUNO
SWORD

Over 150,000 soldiers from the United States, Britain, and Canada stormed the French beaches of Normandy, sparking a surprise attack.

The largest and most dangerous invasion in world history occurred 2 days later on June 6, an event now known as D-Day. That day, the **Allies** landed on the beaches of France. Thousands of American soldiers were killed. But the Nazis were driven back. The Allies **liberated** the French capital of Paris 2 months later and eventually freed all of France from German rule.

The D-Day invasion had a code name. It was "Operation Overlord."

On April 30, 1945, Hitler took his own life. Many claim he did this because he'd rather die than live in fear of being captured.

Meanwhile, U.S. and British bombing attacks were destroying Germany. Some air raids wiped out aircraft production centers. Others rained terror on people in places such as the capital city of Berlin.

Allied troops reached German soil in 1945. Hitler and his Nazi war machine were finished. He had been defeated, pushed back on both sides—the Allies from the West, and the Soviets from the East. Hitler killed himself on April 30, 1945. Seven days later, Germany surrendered. The world was free from the Nazi regime.

U.S. soldiers had helped win the war. But they couldn't have done so without the dedication and sacrifice of the folks at home.

The D-Day Invasion

The most epic event along the Western front during World War II was D-Day. That day, June 6, 1944, was the Allied invasion in France against Nazi German forces. Thousands of American soldiers and those from countries such as Britain and Canada were killed during the landings on the shores of France. Those that faced German gunfire as they rushed onto the beaches have been called the most courageous Americans ever. Can you imagine the bravery it required to know you could easily be killed? Why do you think so many American soldiers risked their lives? Discuss your thoughts with a friend. What do they think?

CHAPTER 3

The Home Front

More than 16 million Americans served in the armed forces during World War II. Their work at home had to be replaced. But those jobs had changed to focus on supporting the war effort. Creating war materials took priority over all other tasks. Materials like metal, paper, and rubber were being sent overseas to help not only the American soldiers but also the Allies. Because of this, Americans had to **ration** basic, but crucial, supplies. It was a massive undertaking. Everyone back home had to work toward a common goal.

The WPB (War Production Board) was an agency that supported war efforts by supervising war production.

Women were encouraged to work to help with the war effort.

Women worked especially hard. While the men were overseas at war, women took over their jobs. Six million worked in defense plants, helping build tanks and planes. Many used much of their pay for childcare. Others were forced to juggle their jobs and duties as mothers. The strain on women was enormous.

More married women than single women entered the workforce during World War II.

Over 20 million victory gardens were planted,
according to the U.S. Department of Agriculture.

The war effort required far more than shifts in the job market. Americans had to also ration other basic necessities like foods such as meat, fish, sugar, and dairy products. Transporting foods, especially fresh food, was limited as tires and gas were also rationed and were being sent overseas to support the military and the Allies. Because of this, many families grew their own vegetables in what were called "victory gardens."

Every household in America was affected by the government's rationing program, which was headed by the Office of Price Administration (OPA). The OPA had volunteers distribute ration books that contained a set number of stamps to be used by families when buying rationed items. The number of stamps the OPA issued to a family depended on the number of people in that family. For instance, families had to turn in a specific stamp for specific items every time they purchased a particular rationed item at the grocery store.

American youth helped as well. They led drives to collect paper, metal, and rubber goods. Their work was vital to the effort. For instance, metal was needed to build tanks and planes.

Such war materials were not just used by American soldiers fighting in Europe. They were also a huge help to those trying to defeat Japan. That front would prove difficult as well.

CHAPTER 4

War in the Pacific

The Japanese attack in Pearl Harbor did more than motivate the United States to enter the war. It severely damaged American naval and air power. It took time for the destroyed ships and planes to be replaced.

This setback allowed the Japanese military time to solidify its hold on Pacific islands that stood between their country and the United States. American forces stood alone. Their Allies, which included Great Britain and France, were busy fighting the Nazis

The plan to attack Pearl Harbor was devised
by Admiral Isoroku Yamamoto.

The Bataan Death March lasted for 6 days.

in Europe. Because of this, the Japanese didn't think the United States would declare war. But it did—the very next day, December 8, 1941. But on December 11, Germany and Italy, who were both Japanese allies, declared war on the United States. The American people were forced into the war in Europe and in the Pacific islands.

The most horrifying event in the Pacific war occurred in April 1942 when the Japanese defeated the Americans in the Philippines. The Japanese forced U.S. prisoners to walk 65 miles (105 kilometers) to the Bataan Peninsula without food or water. The Americans faced disease, starvation, and frequent beatings. About 11,000 died in the Bataan Death March.

The turning point of the war in the Pacific came 2 months later. U.S. forces stopped a Japanese invasion at the U.S. Midway naval base, which guarded Hawaii. American forces then captured islands closer to their enemy. This allowed the United States to send warplanes to bomb Japan.

Only two air raids were needed in 1945 to force Japan to surrender. American planes were loaded with a new weapon called the **atomic** bomb. It was by far the deadliest weapon ever invented.

More U.S. servicemen died in the Air Corps than the Marine Corps.

In August 1945, the United States dropped two atomic bombs on Japan. One was on the city of Hiroshima and the other on the city of Nagasaki. These cities were chosen because they would display just how effective the bomb was. Furthermore, they were industrial cities that contributed to Japan's war effort. This action ended the war. But it caused about 225,000 deaths.

The ugliness of World War II provided a harsh lesson for everyone around the world. People everywhere were in shock over the destruction. The need and desire for peace was felt across the globe. One thing was certain, though. The United States emerged from the war as the greatest military and economic power in the world. An era of **prosperity** in the United States was about to begin.

Still Segregated

African Americans weren't allowed to fight alongside White soldiers during World War II. The U.S. military wouldn't be integrated until 1948. Some Black soldiers fought in their own units with equal skill and bravery. But many were allowed to perform only **menial** labor. They then returned to the United States to the same racism and discrimination they faced before they left. Research the 92nd **Infantry** Division. This was the only African American infantry division to see combat in Europe during World War II. What did you learn? Share your findings with a friend.

World War II was a devastating time in history.

Research & Act

The most tragic outcome of World War II was the Holocaust. During the war, 6 million Jewish people and millions of others were murdered by the Nazis in concentration camps and by other means. But some Jewish people survived and have lived in the United States for generations. Ask your teacher for resources on Holocaust survivors. Read their testimonies. Watch their interviews. Then, discuss the events of the Holocaust with a family member or friend. What questions would you ask these survivors?

Timeline

▶ **March 11, 1941:** Congress passes the Lend-Lease Act, allowing the United States to send war materials to Britain and its Allies.

▶ **December 7, 1941:** The Japanese attack on Pearl Harbor brings the United States into the war.

▶ **December 11, 1941:** The United States declares war on Germany.

▶ **June 4–7, 1942:** The Japanese advance is halted at Midway naval base.

▶ **May 13, 1943:** Allied forces complete victory in the North African campaign.

▶ **August 1943:** Allied forces take over the island of Sicily near Italy.

▶ **June 4, 1944:** Allied troops liberate Rome, Italy.

▶ **June 6, 1944:** D-Day landings begin the push to liberate France and defeat Germany.

▶ **August 25, 1944:** Allied forces liberate Paris, France.

▶ **October 20, 1944:** U.S. troops land in the Philippines.

▶ **May 7, 1945:** Germany surrenders.

▶ **August 6, 1945:** The U.S. military drops the first atomic bomb on Hiroshima, Japan.

▶ **August 9, 1945:** The U.S. military drops the second atomic bomb on Nagasaki, Japan.

▶ **September 2, 1945:** Japan surrenders to officially end World War II.

Further Research

BOOKS

Atkinson, Rick. *D-Day: The Invasion of Normandy, 1944.* New York, NY: Henry Holt and Company, 2014.

Gitlin, Martin. *World War II U.S. Homefront: A History Perspectives Book.* Ann Arbor, MI: Cherry Lake Publishing, 2015.

O'Neill, Bill. *The World War II Trivia Book: Interesting Stories and Random Facts From the Second World War.* CreateSpace Independent Publishing Platform, 2017.

Otfinoski, Steven. *The Split History of the Attack on Pearl Harbor: A Perspectives Flip Book.* North Mankato, MN: Compass Point Books, 2018.

WEBSITE

National Geographic Kids: 10 facts about World War II
https://www.natgeokids.com/uk/discover/history/general-history/world-war-two

Glossary

Allies (AL-eyze) countries fighting alongside the United States in World War II

anti-Semitism (an-tee-seh-muh-tih-zuhm) racist and prejudiced views against Jewish people

atomic (uh-TAH-mik) powered by nuclear energy

conquered (KONG-kuhrd) defeated and assumed control of an enemy

dictator (DIK-tay-tuhr) leader with complete control of a country

fascism (FAH-shih-zuhm) system of government headed by a dictator that allows no opposition

infantry (IN-fuhn-tree) a branch of an army that consists of soldiers trained to fight on foot

internment (in-TUHRN-muhnt) the act of putting someone in prison for political reasons or during war

isolationists (eye-suh-LAY-shuhn-ists) people who want their countries to stay out of foreign affairs

menial (MEE-nee-uhl) lowly

Nazi (NAHT-see) the brutal ruling party of Germany from 1933 to 1945

patriotic (pay-tree-AH-tik) to show a strong love and caring for one's country

prosperity (prah-SPAIR-uh-tee) condition of having financial and material wealth

racism (RAY-sih-zuhm) negative treatment of people because of their race

ration (RAH-shuhn) to control an amount people are allowed to have or use

sacrifice (SAH-kruh-fyss) to give up something for the sake of someone else

Soviet Union (SOH-vee-uht YOON-yuhn) a federation made up of Russia and several other smaller countries

INDEX